'Yes, we did many things, then – all Beautiful . . .'

SAPPHO

Born *c.* 630 BCE, Mytilene, Lesbos
Died *c.* 570 BCE, Mytilene, Lesbos

Taken from Aaron Poochigian's translation of
Stung with Love: Poems and Fragments, first published in 2009.

SAPPHO IN PENGUIN CLASSICS
Stung with Love: Poems and Fragments

SAPPHO

Come Close

Translated by
Aaron Poochigian

PENGUIN BOOKS

PENGUIN CLASSICS

UK | USA | Canada | Ireland | Australia
India | New Zealand | South Africa

Penguin Books is part of the Penguin Random House group of companies
whose addresses can be found at global.penguinrandomhouse.com.

Penguin
Random House
UK

This selection published in Penguin Classics 2015
002

Translation copyright © Aaron Poochigian, 2009

The moral right of the translator has been asserted

Set in 9.5/13 pt Baskerville 10 Pro
Typeset by Jouve (UK), Milton Keynes
Printed in Great Britain by Clays Ltd, St Ives plc

A CIP catalogue record for this book is available from the British Library

ISBN: 978-0-141-39869-3

www.greenpenguin.co.uk

Contents

GODDESSES

Leave Crete and sweep to this blest temple
Where apple-orchard's elegance
Is yours, and smouldering altars, ample
Frankincense.

Here under boughs a bracing spring
Percolates, roses without number
Umber the earth and, rustling,
The leaves drip slumber.

Here budding flowers possess a sunny
Pasture where steeds could graze their fill,
And the breeze feels as gentle as honey . . .

Kypris, here in the present blend
Your nectar with pure festal glee.
Fill gilded bowls and pass them round
Lavishly.

Sweet mother, I can't take shuttle in hand.
There is a boy, and lust
Has crushed my spirit – just
As gentle Aphrodite planned.

Since I have cast my lot, please, golden-crowned
Aphrodite, let me win this round!

Subtly bedizened Aphrodite,
Deathless daughter of Zeus, Wile-weaver,
I beg you, Empress, do not smite me
With anguish and fever

But come as often, on request,
(Hearing me, heeding from afar,)
You left your father's gleaming feast,
Yoked team to car,

And came. Fair sparrows in compact
Flurries of winged rapidity
Cleft sky and over a gloomy tract
Brought you to me –

And there they were, and you, sublime
And smiling with immortal mirth,
Asked what was wrong? why I, this time,
Called you to earth?

What was my mad heart dreaming of? –
'Who, Sappho, at a word, must grow
Again receptive to your love?
Who wronged you so?

'She who shuns love soon will pursue it,
She who scorns gifts will send them still:
That girl will learn love, though she do it
Against her will.'

Come to me now. Drive off this brutal
Distress. Accomplish what my pride
Demands. Come, please, and in this battle
Stand at my side.

'Kytherea, precious
Adonis is nearly dead.
How should we proceed?'

'Come, girls, beat your fists
Down upon your breasts
And shred your dresses.'

A full moon shone,
And around the shrine
Stood devotees
Poised and in place.

Untainted Graces
With wrists like roses,
Please come close,
You daughters of Zeus.

Now, Dika, weave the aniseed together, flower and
    stem,
With your soft hands, crown yourself with a lovely
    diadem
Because the blessèd Graces grant gifts to the garlanded
And snub the worshipper with no flowers on her head.

Come close, you precious
Graces and Muses
With beautiful tresses.

Here is the reason: it is wrong
To play a funeral song
In the Musicians' House –
It simply would not be decorous.

God-crafted product of the tortoise shell,
Come to me; Lyre, be voluble.

He is unrivalled, like a Lesbian
Musician matched with other men.

But when you lie dead
No one will notice later or feel sad
Because you gathered no sprays from the roses
Of the Pierian Muses.

Once lost in Hades' hall
You will be homeless and invisible –
Another shadow flittering back and forth
With shadows of no worth.

DESIRE AND
DEATH-LONGING

That impossible predator,
Eros the Limb-Loosener,
Bitter-sweetly and afresh
Savages my flesh.

Like a gale smiting an oak
On mountainous terrain,
Eros, with a stroke,
Shattered my brain.

But a strange longing to pass on
Seizes me, and I need to see
Lotuses on the dewy banks of Acheron.

That fellow strikes me as god's double,
Couched with you face to face, delighting
In your warm manner, your amiable
Talk and inviting

Laughter – the revelation flutters
My ventricles, my sternum and stomach.
The least glimpse, and my lost voice stutters,
Refuses to come back

Because my tongue is shattered. Gauzy
Flame runs radiating under
My skin; all that I see is hazy,
My ears all thunder.

Sweat comes quickly, and a shiver
Vibrates my frame. I am more sallow
Than grass and suffer such a fever
As death should follow.

But I must suffer further, worthless
As I am . . .

'In all honesty, I want to die.'

Leaving for good after a good long cry,
She said: 'We both have suffered terribly,
But, Sappho, it is hard to say goodbye.'

I said: 'Go with my blessing if you go
Always remembering what we did. To me
You have meant everything, as you well know.

'Yet, lest it slip your mind, I shall review
Everything we have shared – the good times, too:

'You culled violets and roses, bloom and stem,
Often in spring and I looked on as you
Wove a bouquet into a diadem.

'Time and again we plucked lush flowers, wed
Spray after spray in strands and fastened them
Around your soft neck; you perfumed your head

'Of glossy curls with myrrh – lavish infusions
In queenly quantities – then on a bed
Prepared with fleecy sheets and yielding cushions,

'Sated your craving . . .'

May gales and anguish sweep elsewhere
The killer of my character.

But I am hardly some backbiter bent
On vengeance; no, my heart is lenient.

You were at hand,
And I broke down raving –
My craving a fire
That singed my mind,
A brand you quenched.

Cold grew
The spirits of the ladies;
They drew
Their wings close to their bodies.

Moon and the Pleiades go down.
Midnight and tryst pass by.
I, though, lie
Alone.

Peace, you never seemed so tedious
As now – no, never quite like this.

Over eyelids dark night fell
Invisible.

HER GIRLS AND FAMILY

But I love extravagance,
And wanting it has handed down
The glitter and glamour of the sun
As my inheritance.

I truly do believe no maiden that will live
To look upon the brilliance of the sun
Ever will be contemplative
Like this one.

Stand and face me, dear; release
That fineness in your irises.

May you bed down,
Head to breast, upon
The flesh
Of a plush
Companion.

As for you girls, the gorgeous ones,
There will be no change in my plans.

What farm girl, garbed in fashions from the farm
And witless of the way
A hiked hem would display
Her ankles, captivates you with her charm?

. . . off in Sardis
And often turns her thoughts back to our shores.

The girl adored you more than anything,
As if you were a goddess –
But most of all she loved to hear you sing.

Now she outshines those dames with Lydian faces
Just as, when the sun
Has set, the rosy-fingered Moon surpasses

The stars surrounding her. With equal grace
She casts her lustre on
The flower-rich fallows and the sterile seas.

Dew is poured out in handsome fashion; lissome
Chervil unfurls; Rose
And Sweet Clover with heady flowers blossom.

Often on long walks she commemorates
How tender Atthis was.
Her fortune eats at her inconstant thoughts . . .

You will have memories
Because of what we did back then
When we were new at this,

Yes, we did many things, then – all
Beautiful . . .

I loved you once, years ago, Atthis,
When your flower was in place.
You seemed a gawky girl then, artless,
Without grace.

Atthis, you looked at what I was
And hated what you saw
And now, all in a flutter, chase
After Andromeda.

        . . . because
The people I most strive to please
Do me the worst injuries . . .

By giving me creations of their own
My girls have handed me renown.

And this next charming ditty I –
In honour of my girls –
Shall sing out prettily.

Abanthis, please pick up your lyre,
Praise Gongyla. Your need to sing
Flutters about you in the air –
You gorgeous thing.

Her garment (when you stole a glance)
Roused you, and I'm in ecstasy.
Likewise, the goddess Kypris once
Disciplined me

Blaming the way I prayed . . .

As you are dear to me, go claim a younger
Bed as your due.
I can't stand being the old one any longer,
Living with you.

Girls, chase the violet-bosomed Muses' bright
Gifts and the plangent lyre, lover of hymns:

Stiffness has seized on these once supple limbs,
And black braids with the passing years turned white.

Age weighs heavily on me, and the knees
Buckle that long ago, like fawns, pranced nimbly.

I groan much but to what end? Humans simply
Cannot be ageless like divinities.

They say that rosy-forearmed Dawn, when stung
With love, swept a sweet youth to the earth's rim –

Tithonous. Even there age withered him,
Bound still to a wife forever young.

Kypris, may Doricha discover
You are the bitterest thing of all
And not keep boasting that a lover
Twice came to call.

Nereids, Kypris, please restore
My brother to this port, unkilled.
May all his heart most wishes for
Now be fulfilled.

Excuse the misdeeds in his past,
Make him his friends' boon and foes' bane,
And may we never find the least
Cause to complain.

May he choose to give his sister
Her share of honour but my gloomy
Misgivings . . .

I have a daughter who reminds me of
A marigold in bloom.
Kleïs is her name,
And I adore her.
I would refuse all Lydia's glitter for her
And all other love.

I do not have an
Ornately woven
Bandeau to hand you,
Kleïs. From
Where would it come?

. . . You see, my mother,

Back when she was young,
Thought it was fancy for a girl to wear
A purple fillet, a headband –

Yes, this was quite the thing.
Now, though, we have seen a girl with hair
More orange than a firebrand

Sport all the flowers of spring
Woven together, garlands upon garlands –
And only lately, fresh from Sardis,

A spangled headband . . .

Mnasis sent you from Phocaia
Purple kerchiefs you can tie
Around your brow to serve
As headscarves, too –
Rich gifts which you,
With your fine cheeks, deserve.

A handkerchief
Dripping with . . .

TROY

Idaos, then, the panting emissary,
Reported:
       'Out of Asia deathless glory:
From holy Thebe and the stream-fed port
Of Plakia, Hector and his men escort
The bright-eyed, delicate Andromache
On shipboard over the infertile sea –
With sweet red garments, bracelets made of gold,
Beautiful baubles, ivory and untold
Chalices chased in silver.' So he spoke.

Dear Priam rose at once, and the news broke,
Spreading to friends throughout the city's wide
Expanse. And soon the sons of Ilos tied
Pack mules to smooth-wheeled carts, and whole
    parades
Clambered aboard the transports – wives and maids
With slim-tapering ankles. Some way off,
The daughters of King Priam stood aloof,
And youthful stewards harnessed teams of horses
To chariots . . .

. . . And sweetly then the double-oboe's cadence
Mingled with rhythmic rattles as the maidens
Sang sacred songs. A fine sound strode the air.
Cups on the roadside, vessels everywhere,
Cassia and frankincense were mixed with myrrh.
Old women (venerable as they were)
Warbled and trilled. The men all in a choir
Summoned first that lover of the lyre,
The long-range archer, Paeon, then extolled
Andromache and Hector, godlike to behold.

Some call ships, infantry or horsemen
The greatest beauty earth can offer;
I say it is whatever a person
Most lusts after.

Showing you all will be no trouble:
Helen surpassed all humankind
In looks but left the world's most noble
Husband behind,

Coasting off to Troy where she
Thought nothing of her loving parents
And only child but, led astray . . .

. . . and I think of Anaktoria
Far away, . . .

And I would rather watch her body
Sway, her glistening face flash dalliance
Than Lydian war cars at the ready
And armed battalions.

Yes, you have all heard
That Leda, long ago, one day
Noticed an egg, hyacinth-coloured,
Hidden away.

Reveal your graceful figure here,
Close to me, Hera. I make entreaty
Just as the kings once made their prayer,
The famous Atreidai –

Winning victories by the score
At Troy first, then at sea, they sailed
The channel to this very shore,
Tried leaving but failed

Until they prayed to you, the Saviour
Zeus and Thyone's charming son.
Like long ago, then, grant this favour,
As you have done . . .

MAIDENS AND
MARRIAGES

Sappho

Once as a too, too lissome
Maiden was plucking a blossom . . .

Artemis made the pledge no god can break:
'Upon my head and all that I hold dear,
I shall remain a maid, a mountaineer
Hunting on summits – grant this for my sake.'

The Father of the Blessèd gave the nod – yes;
And all the gods pronounced her Frontier Goddess
And Slayer of Stags, and Eros never crosses
Her path . . .

(I)

A ripe red apple grows, the highest of them all,
Over the treetop, way up on a tapering spray,
But apple-gatherers never see it – no,
Rather, they *do* see it is far away,
Beyond their reach, impossible.
This matter stands just so.

(II)

A hillside hyacinth shepherds treaded flat,
A red bloom in the dust – it is like that.

'Maidenhead, maidenhead, where have you gone?'

'I shall never, ever join you again.'

Hesperus, you are
The most fetching star.
What Dawn flings afield
You bring back together –
Sheep to the fold, goats to the pen,
And the child to his mother again.

Nightingale,
All you sing
Is desire;
You are the crier
Of coming spring.

Because once on a time you were
Young, sing of what is taking place,
Talk to us for a spell, confer
Your special grace.

For we march to a wedding – yes,
You know it well. So pack the maids off
Quickly, and may the gods possess . . .

Groomsmen, kings with bastions
In strong positions,
Keep this bride
Well fortified.

It would take seven fathoms to span
The feet of the doorkeeper (the best man);
His sandals are five cows' worth of leather
And ten shoemakers stitched them together.

'What do you resemble, dear husband-to-be?'

'You resemble a supple seedling, a green tree.'

> Carpenters, raise the rafter-beam
> (For Hymen's wedding hymn)
> A little higher to make room
> (For Hymen's wedding hymn)
> Because here comes the groom –
> An Ares more imposing than
> A giant, a terribly big man.

Blest bridegroom, this day of matrimony,
Just as you wished it, has come true:
The bride is whom you wished for . . .

                          'You

Move gracefully; your eyes are honey;
Charm was showered on your radiant face –
Yes, Aphrodite granted you outstanding praise.'

The ambrosial mixture
Ready in the mixing bowl,
Hermes went round with a pitcher
And served the gods. When all
Had tipped their goblets and poured offerings,
They prayed that the groom suffer only the good
    things.

Because there is no other girl than she,
Bridegroom – a child still, of such quality.

Star clusters near the fair moon dim
Their shapely shimmering whenever
She rises, lucent to the brim
And flowing over.

Sappho

And may the maidens all night long
Celebrate your shared love in song
And the bride's bosom,
A violet-blossom.

Get up, now! Rouse that gang of fellows –
Your boys – and we shall sleep as well as
The bird that intones
Piercing moans.

THE WISDOM OF
SAPPHO

The gorgeous man presents a gorgeous view;
The good man will in time be gorgeous, too.

> Wealth without real worthiness
> Is no good for the neighbourhood;
> But their proper mixture is
> The summit of beatitude.

Neither the honey nor the bee
For me . . .

'I want to tell you something but good taste
Restrains me.'
                            'If you wanted to express
Some noble or gorgeous thought – that is, unless
Your tongue were keen to utter in hot haste
Some shameful slur, "good taste" would not have
     dressed
Your face in red, no, you would have professed
Whatever you would say upfront and straightaway.'

Either I have slipped out of your head
Or you adore some fellow more, instead.

I don't know what the right course is;
Twofold are my purposes.

I declare
That later on,
Even in an age unlike our own,
Someone will remember who we are.